# I'm ROOTING for You

I'm **R** O O T I N G for you

I'm R **O** O T I N G for you

I'm R O **O** T I N G for you

I'm R O O **T** I N G for you

I'm R O O T **I** N G for you

I'm R O O T I **N** G for you

I'm R O O T I N **G** for you

# TABLE OF CONTENTS

Session One: PURPOSE
Session Two: HEALTH
Session Three: FAITH
Session Four: FEARLESS
Session Five: DISCIPLINE

Session Six: SELF ESTEEM
Session Seven: SELF REGULATION
Session Eight: STRETCHING YOURSELF
Session Nine: FOCUS
Session Ten: HOPE

Session Eleven: COURAGE
Session Twelve: STRENGTH
Session Thirteen: LOVE
Session Fourteen: PEACE
Session Fifteen: JOY

Session Sixteen: FAMILY UNITY
Session Seventeen: BUILDING CHARACTERS
Session Eighteen: PRINCIPLES
Session Nineteen: RESTORATION
Session Twenty: BALANCE

# Purpose

Define **purpose**:_____
_____
_____
_____
_____
_____

As Christians, we have the added_____and _____in knowing that God is with us in our struggles and can use our pain to bless others. Take time to reflect on your own personal pain and how you can use it to inspire and encourage others. Struggles aren't prejudice.

Regardless of your fame, fortune, or abilities, life is filled with_____. You get to choose how you will react to those_____. Learning to deal with them in healthy, productive ways will result in personal growth and peace of mind. Being willing to endure the space between the initial pain and the healing of it, is where you will grow the most.

Your struggles may hold the key to your true calling in life.

If you were to critique yourself, what is your greateststruggle currently?
_____
_____
_____

___
___
___

Here is where we will outline **FOUR** healthy and effective approaches to coping with the struggles of life:

One: Eliminating overthinking.
How are you an OVER THINKER?

_____
_____
_____
_____
_____
_____

Two: Working from your strengths.
Have you IDENTIFIED your strengths?

_____
_____
_____
_____
_____
_____

Three: Taking time for self-care.
What does SELF CARE look like to you?

_____
_____
_____
_____
_____
_____

Four: Finding meaning in your experiences What have your experiences TAUGHT you?

# Health

GOD is our healer. It is essential to recognize that healing is not just something that GOD does but is a major part of who HE is. This means that our faith should not be in the act of healing but rather in GOD, the Healer.

## How does GOD heal us

Mentally:

Physically:

Emotionally:

Financially:

Spiritually:

Healing is complete. When symptoms reappear, it is crucial not to accept them, as sickness is not your identity.

Let us declare that you are a healthy person fighting sickness and not a sick person trying to get healthy.

It is important to note that some people may lose their healing. How?

_____
_____
_____
_____
_____
_____
_____

Is faith required for healing?

_____
_____
_____
_____
_____
_____
_____

The key to keeping that healing is by keeping your _____ in the Healer and maintaining your _____ of. _____

# Faith

Faith is not about you believing it will happen.......ONLY. It's about you knowing that_____have been made for that healing to manifest.

Trusting in God to manifest. Trusting in GOD to manifest every promise made. Knowing that HE is not a man that, HE could lie.

Though GOD is able to manifest HIS promises, we have free will. GOD gave us free will so that we would never be forced to do HIS will.

Faith is a free_____that we choose to exercise. Let's repeat this, faith is a free_____that we choose to exercise.

When we let go of our will and allow GOD's will be done, we get to live a life of manifested promises. Having faith in _____and being obedient to the will of _____is the key to manifesting the blessed life.

We must be willing to obey the word of GOD that we believe. We must be willing to obey the word of GOD that we know.

What would a BLESSED LIFE look like to you?
_____
_____
_____
_____
_____
_____
_____
_____
_____
_____
_____

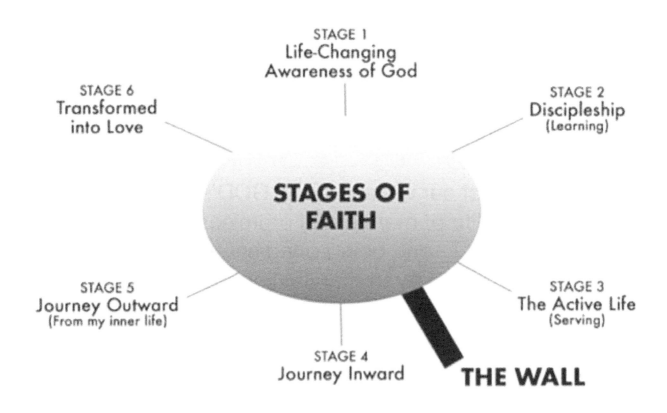

What stage of FAITH are you currently in? Stage _____

# Fearless

When the Holy Spirit resides within you, you are both _____ and fearless in that very moment.

Define fearless in your own words:

_____
_____
_____
_____
_____
_____

Being fearless means embracing a mindset of courage, embracing resilience, and embracing freedom from the constraints of fear. Oftentimes, we entertain things we should be embracing.

When you embrace the truth of GOD, it involves stepping outside of your comfort zone, taking risks, and facing challenges head-on without allowing fear to dictate your actions or limit your potential.

What areas of your life have fear resided? One

_____
_____
_____
_____
_____
_____

Second

# A Bold Declaration

I declare – That *I am blessed* with God's supernatural wisdom, and I have clear direction for my life.

I declare – That *I am blessed* with creativity, with courage, with ability, and with abundance.

I declare – *I am blessed* with a strong will and with self-control and self-discipline.

I declare – That *I am blessed* with a great family, with good friends, with good health, and with faith, favor, and fulfillment.

I declare – That *I am blessed* with success, with supernatural strength, with promotion, and with divine protection.

I declare – That *I am blessed* with an obedient heart and with a positive outlook on life.

I declare – That any curse that has been spoken over me, any negative evil word that has ever come against me, is broken right now.

I declare – That *I am blessed* in the city. *I am blessed* in the country. *I am blessed* when I go in. *I am blessed* when I come out.

I declare – That everything I put my hands to do is going to prosper and succeed.

#fearless

# Discipline

_____ often comes off as negative, especially from the world's view. Having discipline with the Lord is good.

Applicable discipline leads to a fulfilling and good _____ The Lord has the power to restore your health and allow you to live fully. Even though anguish can be difficult to bear, it is often good for us in the long run, as it leads to growth and development.

# Define anguish:

_____
_____
_____
_____
_____

Anguish can manifest both physically and emotionally. You must be in tune with your body and emotions. When those feelings are not worked through internally, they will begin to show externally. Physically, this can create bodily sensations, including pain, soreness, heaviness, tearfulness, and slowed movement and momentum.

Have you experienced any of these physical signs of ANGUISH?
If so, which ones?, _____, _____

Take care of yourself; you only get ONE you…..

Through God's _____ and _____, we have been rescued from death and forgiven of all our sins. Therefore, keeping our hearts clean from sin and confessing our transgressions to receive healing is important.

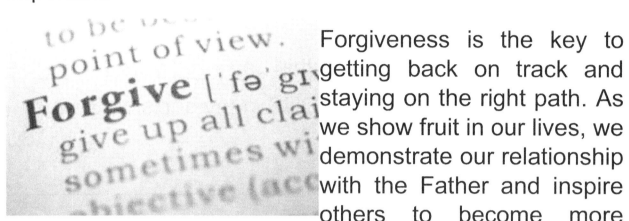

Forgiveness is the key to getting back on track and staying on the right path. As we show fruit in our lives, we demonstrate our relationship with the Father and inspire others to become more disciplined and fruitful as well.

If you find yourself stuck:

1. Practice empathy…
2. Ask yourself about the circumstances that may have led the other person to behave in such a way…..
3. Reflect on times when others have forgiven you.
4. Write in a journal, pray, or use guided meditation……
5. Be aware that forgiveness is a process

**Remember** that with **the Lord on our side,** we can confidently face any challenge that comes our way. Declare that over yourself….

Your Declaration to FORGIVE:

I,_____ on this day (___) year (_____), declare that I will be VICTORIOUS in my decision to forgive:

_____
_____
_____
_____
_____
_____
_____
_____
_____
_____
_____
_____
_____
_____
_____
_____
_____
_____
_____

_____
Signed

# Self-Esteem

Self-esteem is confidence in one's own worth, abilities, or morals.

Self-esteem encompasses beliefs about oneself as well as emotional states, such as
_____,_____,_____, and_____.

Based on our opinions and beliefs about ourselves, which can feel difficult to embrace and sometimes challenging to.

## Let's talk about LOW SELF-ESTEEM.

Low self-esteem can reduce the quality of a person's life in many different ways, including negative feelings.

The constant self-criticism can lead to persistent feelings of:

_____

_____

_____

_____

_____

When you feel like this, your tank is low or empty.

Self-confidence is the emotional component of your personality and the most important factor in determining how you _____, and _____.

Your level of self-confidence largely determines what you make happen in life. When you are confident, **your tank is full.**

The first step to true confidence is looking at God's Word. God encourages us to check our thoughts and actions when dealing with our self-esteem.
We must find our confidence and self-esteem in His abilities and what He has done for us, in us, and through us. This means we must stop leaning on our understanding of value and worth.

Define value:_____
_____

Define worth:_____
_____

The world says you have value if you work hard enough, and it's based on your own abilities. God's Word says a very different thing. GOD says we are made in HIS image; therefore, we have value. Genesis 1:27

**Confidence** is a trait that enables one to stand firm in the face of adversity.

In a world filled with wars, politics, racism, _____ ___, illness, drug addictions, poverty, worldwide sickness, and family issues, having an anchor source is crucial.

When we are planted with God, our life is filled with _____, _____, _____, and faith.

As children, we trusted our parents to provide for us financially, physically, and mentally. Similarly, we can have total confidence in God our Father as our source of provision. Define provision: _____
_____
_____
_____
_____
_____

He will continue to water us as we grow in Him. Our knowledge, wisdom, and will should be infused with the assurance of the Lord, producing action. Trusting in our own understanding is limited, but when we trust in God, our roots of confidence and trust are nourished by the stream of life found in Him. Anyone can trust that the Lord will do what He has promised. However, those who trust solely in the Lord have a spiritual maturity that allows them to leave the outcome of their situation in God's capable hands without expecting anything in return. What is GOD capable of in your life? Be specific:

_____

_____

_____

_____

Today, stand firm that your source of all blessings is in the Lord.

# Self Regulation

Here is a BIG THOUGHT:

It is believed that all the_____,_____, and agents that lead to temptation are under the control of God. God knows what His people are capable of_____, and HE has complete control over all that can affect them.

In order to control ourselves, we must practice self-regulation.

Define SELF REGULATION:

_____
_____
_____

By allowing the power of the Holy Spirit within us, we are able to possess self-control and demonstrate the fruits of the Spirit. Let's go, Bible!!! What are the fruits of the Spirit. Galatians 5:22-23

1. _____
2. _____
3. _____
4. _____
5. _____
6. _____
7. _____
8. _____
9. _____

Note: WE ARE ABLE TO POSSESS SELF CONTROL

Self-control allows us to live in a way that is pleasing to God rather than giving in to our sinful nature.

**Self-regulation** also enables us to activate the parasympathetic nervous system, which facilitates\_\_\_and _____after experiencing stress. YOU MUST WATCH HOW STRESS IS AFFECTING YOU. By learning to regulate ourselves and to manage our stress, we can better manage life and life's responses. This level of management leads to healthier and more balanced lives. Eventually, we will begin to see the positive impact of self-regulation in our homes, schools, churches, and workplaces.

S - Silencing

Have you learned how to **silence** the noises outside of you?

T - Taking

You are **taking** on other people's problems or dilemmas!

R - Risking

Are you taking **risks** that you haven't prayed over or sought wisdom for?

E - Extending

Are you **extending** yourself beyond your peace?

S - Staying

You must know when **staying** is no longer a win for you!

S - Separating

Knowing when you must **separate** yourself from chaos, violence, or stress!

# Stretching Yourself

When an individual commits to stretching themselves, it is stretching internally and not physically. Most initially think of
_____ or some external expression of stretching. When you are of that mindset, you most possibly push yourself too far. However, today, there is a message that God has for you.

GOD desires to heal you and to see that you can be stretched for the kingdom.

With everything that is happening in the world, more and more people will be turning to Christ. More people will be seeking the things of the Kingdom.

## Let's Talk Gifts

The gifts that God has given you are meant to uplift the kingdom.

Throughout his letters, Apostle Paul mentions several spiritual gifts: wisdom, faith, discernment, teaching, administration, service, mercy, hospitality, and encouragement.

Every believer has gifts. Which of these do you have?

_____

_____

_____

_____

_____

# GOD GIVES GIFTS

You will need to have spiritual boldness to not hold back and to fully operate in your God-given gifts.

God is not asking you to move anxiously or to be stretched for where you are; instead, you will be asked to support others working in the kingdom.
Remember, you do have a choice to use your gifts, but it is a benefit and not a curse to advance them with tools for the Kingdom.

As you draw closer to God, He will heal you from the inside out, and as a result, you will be laying the foundations for beneficial blessings for the generations behind you. So stretch yourself for God and see how He enlarges your territory.

*notes*

Here are some questions to ponder. How much more of yourself can you give? Where are you holding back?
What area is GOD stretching you in?

Taking the time to answer these questions is VITAL. You need to be able to identify what areas you are being stretched in.

When you understand where you are being stretched, you will no longer see the areas you are being stretched as areas where you are being defeated.

# FOCUS

We all need to be aware of the idea that _____ can take many forms.

Distractions can lead us off track. It's important to recognize the things that distract us and interrupt our focus in life.

What are three things that are distractions for you?
1. _____
2. _____
3. _____

When we are aligned with God_____
_____, it's important to be aware that the enemy may try to_____us. Define derail: _____
_____

> Our impact on the lives of others can bring light to a dark world. If we want healing and victory, we need to slow down, tune out the noise of life, and invite God into our lives. Rather than running around aimlessly, we need to focus on God and listen for His still, small voice. God wants our attention so that He can reveal the plan He has for our lives. We must rest in the fact that He wants to give us hope, healing, and a bright future, but we must be paying attention. The battles we face are battles of light against darkness and good against evil, and God fights them for us.

We must take time to be still and pay attention to God, for this is a war!

Psalm 46:10

Be still, and know that I am God: I will be exalted among the heathen; I will be exalted in the earth.

# Focus on your goals

*I'm Rooting For You*

## Stay Focused on Your Goals

**CREATE AN EVENING ROUTINE**

Timing is everything when you have a goal. You can use time to your advantage and make each day a little easier.

**WRITE YOUR GOALS DOWN**

Writing down your goals makes them real. Once this happens, you have to deal with them.

**PLAN YOUR DAY**

It's so much easier to complete everything you need to do in a day when you have a clear plan. Write out all your must-do's in your planner as well as your "hope to do's."

@sophiamscott

@sophiascott

# HOPE

Hope is a state of mind that is both_____and _____.

Based on the expectation of good outcomes in events and circumstances in one's life or the world. Our hope can be built on our_____and _____, and God is often referred to as the "God of Hope," the ultimate source of real hope.

Letting go and letting God can bring many blessings into our lives. Holding on to things beyond it's expiration date is derailing to real life and success. You must know when to LET GO and when to LET GOD!

Let go *and* let God.

When we are healing, it's essential to have hope and a vision of our recovery to embrace it fully.

God wants to give us a clear vision of who He is and His plans for us. Have you received a VISION from GOD?

_____
_____
_____

This vision from GOD is wisdom, guiding us through the good and the bad times. Having a clear vision helps us avoid being influenced by others who may not have our best interests at heart.

By following God's vision, we can live the abundant life that He intends for us. If we don't know where we're going, we can't expect others to follow us. Let's open our eyes and visualize a healthy, hopeful future.

_____
_____
_____

## Scriptures of HOPE:

Write 5 scriptures that focus on HOPE

Scripture One:
_____
_____
_____

Scripture Two:
_____
_____
_____

Scripture Three:
_____
_____
_____

Scripture Four:
_____
_____
_____

Scripture Five:
_____
_____
_____

# Courage

God has a tendency to_____with individuals who are active in their pursuits. When Jesus was tasked with selecting his disciples, he sought out individuals who were already actively engaged in their work.

Who were they?

_____ _____ _____

_____ _____ _____

_____ _____ _____

True courage is not just a_____; it is an_____ God wants us to not only have courage in the things of this world but also in our spiritual pursuits. Everyone has work that they are called to do, even when we don't see or feel like the task is meant for us.

Courage is the ability to: _____

_____

With God's protection and guidance, we should be able to conquer our fears and live a life full of determination. God commands us to have courage, which means having faith and confidence in Him. Through scripture, we can find the courage that God desires us to have. As we walk in God's _____and He elevates us, He will reveal the true intentions of those around us. This is to show us who is genuine and who is just playing from a distance. When we are healing from the inside out, we have the choice and willingness to confront_____,_____,_____,

_____, or intimidation. The word "courage" shares a root with the French word coeur or heart. So when we act with courage, we're acting from the heart, from our inner instincts.

**Courage is an essential……**

# A Courageous Prayer:

Dear Father,

I pray that you grant me the courage to stand firm in my faith and remain anchored to the unalterable Word of God.

Please protect me from spiritual deception and grant me the wisdom to recognize the enemy's tactics to dilute the message of the gospel.

Please wash my mind with the cleansing power of the Word of Truth and help me put on the whole armor of God so that I may stand firm in the evil day. I humbly ask all these things in Jesus' name. Amen.

**What areas do you need to stand firm in?**

1. _____
2. _____
3. _____
4. _____
5. _____
6. _____

In Jesus Name, Amen

## Strength

Your strengths are the qualities and abilities that make you successful.

Believe in yourself and use your strength to fuel your goals. What are two areas of proof that you have to show that you believe in yourself?

One: _____
_____
_____

Two: _____
_____
_____

**True strength** isn't just about how much weight you can hold; it's about how you handle the weight. What does that statement mean to you?

_____
_____
_____

Use your struggles as fuel to achieve your goals and push through_____. Push through them all.

**As believers**, we must fight for what we want in life, even when there are people or limiting beliefs standing in our way. Don't give up on what you want; it may be just one reach away. Remember, your strengths are the qualities and abilities that make you successful.

Lord, I pray not for tranquility nor that my tribulations may cease; I pray for your spirit and your love that you grant me strength and grace to overcome adversity through Jesus Christ. Amen.
Selah

# Love

Luke 6:35 NIV:

"But love your enemies, do good to them, and lend to them without expecting to get anything back. Then your reward will be great, and you will be children of the Most High because he is kind to the ungrateful and wicked."

**Love** comes in various forms and types, but the most powerful and rewarding love is Agape love, which originates from God. It is a selfless love that is given without any expectations of receiving anything in return.

**Agape love** is the_____level of love that one can offer. It is a conscious decision to spread love in all circumstances, including those that are destructive. As we strive to become more like God, our character will reflect Agape love more easily.

Negative people and enemies surround us. They surround us every day in some way. How should love manifest itself in these moments? _____
_____
_____
_____

It's often those who are closest to us that hurt us the most. Moving forward, how will you respond to a loved one not being loving? _____

_____
_____
_____

God desires your heart today. Your full heart. Not holding back.

Can you trust GOD to protect your heart and to keep your peace? _____

**GOD** wants to heal you. HE wants to heal your wounds, scars, and dark corners of your heart and clean out the closet of your heart.

**GOD** has a few areas in your heart that He wants to heal.

**Forgiveness**

**Bitterness**

**Grief**

**Envy,**

**Jealousy**

**Slander**

**Adultery**

**Idolatry**

**Theft**

**Deceit**

How will you know when you are healed in a particular area?
_____
_____
_____

If you have ever experienced a love that is not easily broken, like that of a parent, child, pet, long-lasting friendship, or marriage, God wants that with you. As you open your heart to God, He will mend the pieces of your heart and make you more like Him, showing **Agape love.**

Write out one instance where you showed **Agape love:**

_____
_____
_____

# Peace

The passage you provided speaks about achieving a fulfilling life by following God's plan for us. It encourages us to rest in the fact that everything will be alright when we trust in God. The invitation is to receive rest as a form of peace, which is something many people may not have experienced before.

We are often guilty of overthinking things when God has already given us a plan and purpose to achieve. Don't overthink it. Overthinking causes us to doubt the plan and purpose of GOD.

Define OVERTHINKING:
_____
_____
_____
_____

The outline for life's greatest journey can be found **in the Bible.**

The invitation in this passage is for those who are burdened with the guilt of sin and are seeking spiritual rest. This rest can be found through an application of _____, a view of free justification by the_____of Christ and full compensation of sin by His sacrifice.

The passage concludes by encouraging us to place our burdens on the Lord so that we can have a more fulfilling life.

What burden do you need to place on the Lord?

_____
_____
_____

# A Prayer of Peace

Dear Heavenly Father,

I want to thank You for providing a way for me to come close to You by removing the barrier of sin. I long to be close and to be in communion with you, Father.

I am grateful that You offer true rest for my soul and you give perfect peace for my heart and that even in the midst of life's storms. Your peace will always remain.

I humbly ask that You show mercy to those who have not yet come to know You. Please convict their hearts and help them see their need for salvation and the redemption that comes through trusting in Your blood. This is our prayer.


In Jesus' name, Amen.

# Joy

It appears that in order to experience healing in life, one must reach a point where they are fed up with being sick and tired.

Are you sick and tired? _____

Many people simply endure their struggles without taking any action. However, true _____can only occur once we reach this breaking point. Transformation involves a significant_____in appearance or form.

Major events such as getting a driver's license, going to college, starting a family, or getting married can all lead to transformations in our lives. What is another major event in your life? _____

_____

_____These changes are often extreme and can be challenging to navigate.

We need to identify what is preventing us from achieving our goals. Do you know what is holding you back? _____
Is there something keeping you from becoming the best you? _____

Sometimes, we may be blind to our own shortcomings and need to take a hard look at ourselves. Change can be painful, but it is necessary in order to grow. We need to confront the things that are holding us back and embrace the discomfort that comes along with it.

God has promised us joy and healing, but we must be willing to mourn in order to experience it. We need to come to terms with our sins and recognize our lack of righteousness. When we are humble and recognize our shortcomings, we can begin to heal and move forward. God takes our mourning and transforms it into dancing, turning our sorrow into joy.

Prosperity is both a gift and a test, and it is important to remain rooted in God in both good times and bad

Let's discuss areas of ANGER.

We must remember that God is not only gracious but also righteously angry. The difference between our anger and GOD's anger is that His anger serves his favor and ultimately leads to our healing. We need to praise God with our whole being, including our mind, heart, voice, and body. All of us.
Jesus has conquered the grave, and we can trust that joy will have the last laugh. Our confidence is in Jesus always having the victory.

Are you operating in anger wrongly?
_____
_____
_____
_____
_____

Give us two specifics that you gave over to

unrighteous anger:

One:


_____
_____
_____
_____
_____

Two:
_____
_____
_____
_____
_____

# Family Unity

1 John 4:20-21 MSG:

"20-21 If anyone boasts, **"I love God,"** and goes right on hating his brother or sister, thinking nothing of it, he is a liar. If he won't love the person he can see, how can he love the God he can't see? The command we have from Christ is blunt: Loving God includes loving people. You've got to love both."

The importance of **building strong character** is often first taught in the home, where families form a generational foundation of unity and love. Unfortunately, in modern times, it is becoming more common for people to become disconnected from their families. It is through a loving parental relationship that sets an example for the family that a strong sense of unity and cohesion is built, extending in a personal way to each child. A strong family relationship is built on Christian values, and today, God is reminding us to love people and not just Him. God's outline for us to follow is key to becoming better individuals and family members.

What are some Christian values that you have implemented in your family?

_____
_____
_____

The enemy dislikes family unity and seeks to create separations in our lives through wounds, pride, and pain.

We must strive to walk in humility and let the Lord reveal our_____ so that we can turn and be free. Pride is a number one killer. When you operate in pride, you lose humility. Humility creates an atmosphere around our lives that is toxic to separation, and it is through unity that we can defeat the enemy in his attempts to destroy our relationships with our families and with God.

Unity is key to the success of the family

# How to build a strong character

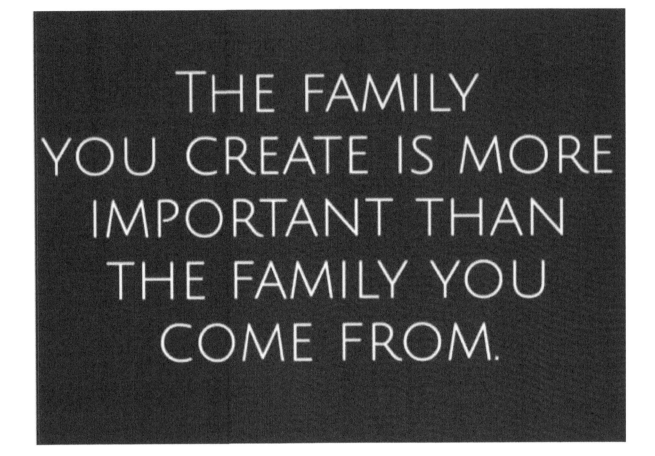

What are seven building blocks that you use:

1. _____
2. _____
3. _____
4. _____
5. _____
6. _____
7. _____

# Principles

Principles refer to a fundamental truth or proposition that forms the basis of a system of belief or behavior. Define the principle in your own words:

_____
_____
_____

In today's world, individuals have different principles that they stand by. One acquires these principles from various sources such as upbringing,
school
college
friends
religious background,
family history.

These principles shape an individual's character and guide them on how to live and interact with others. To develop sound principles, one needs to be curious about the world around them. The world has many principles that it stands on, including material gain, physical beauty, and pride, among others. However, seeking a fulfilling life requires an individual to turn towards Christ.

The Bible provides long-lasting principles that guide one on how to live a fulfilling life. These principles include_____, _____, selflessness, and_____, among others. Embracing these principles leads to a healed and fulfilled life. It is essential to evaluate the principles that one stands on and determine if they lead to a fulfilled life. By aligning oneself with God's principles, one can live a life filled with joy, contentment, and purpose.

Align your life with GOD's principles. You deserve a rooted life.

How to apply PRINCIPLES

Where can you find the principles of GOD? You can find the principles of GOD in the word of GOD.

What are 3 principles you have found in the word of GOD:

Principle Number One:
_____
_____
_____

Principle Number Two:
_____
_____
_____

Principle Number Three:
_____
_____
_____

# Restoration

**Restoration** is the process of returning to the way God initially created you, not to your previous state before you were exposed. A **new heart** is a remarkable thing. There is a **fresh** heart that is received at the moment of salvation. However, there is also a process of that **new heart** growing to be like **Christ's** heart.

When you are genuinely healed, it becomes easier to interact with society. You realize your worth in God. When this occurs, it should not come as a surprise when people or groups that influenced you or had connections with you either step back or maintain a distance. Not everyone can handle your accomplished life's purpose. Now that God has healed you from within, the battle continues. The enemy knows you have been cured.
Everything has an anticipated conclusion.

Since you have been healed, it is now simpler to follow the Lord's ways and resist the enticements of the adversary. In the words of Israel Houghton's "Moving Forward" song, "I'm not going back; I'm moving ahead. I'm here to announce to you that your past is over; all things are made new. I surrender my life to Christ, and I'm moving forward." Move forward today, recognizing that God has the final say!

**Our Prayer:**
Dear God, I want to thank You for being the God of all grace and for sending Your Son, Jesus Christ, to suffer for us on the Cross. I am grateful that through His sacrifice, my sins

have been forgiven, and the chains of sin and Satan in my life have been broken. Please continue to perfect, confirm, strengthen, and establish me in my faith, and help me to always remember that You have started a good work in me and will continue until the day of Christ Jesus. Thank You for Your love and grace, and may I always honor You in my thoughts, words, and actions. In Jesus' name, I pray. Amen. Selah

# Balanced

As you continue to live the fulfilled life that God has called you to, you will begin to see the greater purpose. It is important to maintain a balanced life while being in this world, but not of it.

Your integrity will reflect your balance.

Always stand firm on God's eternal principles and the ones that you have recently learned. Whenever you feel unbalanced, take action by talking to God, reading your word, seeking wisdom from a mentor or therapist, and revisiting this journal. When you are balanced, your circle of influence will be strengthened. Remember, God loves unity. Unity honors the many names for God, the many paths to God, and the many ways to worship God, for there is only one power and presence of God, and He loves us all equally.

Homeostasis is an essential process that helps a living organism maintain internal stability while adapting to changing external conditions.

In your own words, define homeostasis:

_____
_____
_____

It is not fixed or unchanging but rather a dynamic process that can respond to external challenges. **By healing from**

**the inside,** it becomes easier to heal on the outside. Always remember that what you do in private with God will reward you publicly. So, let your light shine and celebrate yourself, and don't allow anything to steal your joy! From this moment forward, DON'T ALLOW ANYTHING TO STEAL YOUR JOY.

**I'm Rooting For You**

**Behold, [in the restored Jerusalem] I will bring to it health and healing, and I will heal them; and I will reveal to them an abundance of peace (prosperity, security, stability) and truth.**

*Signed,*
Sophia Scott

Made in the USA
Middletown, DE
20 May 2025

75724621R00038